THE LOVE POEMS

Books by John Montague
published by
Exile Editions

SELECTED POEMS

THE DEAD KINGDOM

MOUNT EAGLE

JOHN MONTAGUE

The Love Poems

drawings by

CLAIRE WEISSMAN WILKS

TORONTO
Exile Editions
1992

This Edition is published by Exile Editions Ltd.,
20 Dale Avenue, Toronto, Ontario, Canada M4W 1K4

Sales distribution
General Publishing Co. Ltd.
30 Lesmill Road, Don Mills, Ontario M3B 2T6

Designed by LOU LUCIANI
Typeset in STEMPEL GARAMOND
Printed in Canada by UNIVERSITY OF TORONTO PRESS

ISBN 1-55096-088-1

The translations
after the French of André Frénaud
are by John and Evelyn Montague

CONTENTS

Rooms

~

Return

~

Love, A Greeting

~

Tracks

~

Discords

Stoney Plain, Honey Field

~

Allegiances

~

She Speaks

~

Blessing

A feel of warmth in this place.
In winter air, a scent of harvest.
No form of prayer is needed,
When by sudden grace attended.
Naturally, we fall from grace.
Mere humans, we forget what light
Led us, lonely, to this place.

Rooms

Through rooms I wandered
in search of the Beloved,
a candlelight always further away ...

Once we found each other
in a close and breathing darkness,
the warmth abides to this day ...

AFTER THE ARABIC

THE SAME GESTURE

There is a secret room
of golden light where
everything – love, violence,
hatred is possible;
and, again love.

Such intimacy of hand
and mind is achieved
under its healing light
that the shifting of
hands is a rite

like court music.
We barely know our
selves there though
it is what we always were
– most nakedly are –

and must remember
when we leave, re-
suming our habits
with our clothes:
work, 'phone, drive

through late traffic
changing gears with
the same gesture as
eased your snowbound
heart and flesh.

DO NOT DISTURB

A shaft rising towards
or falling from, love.
Caressing glances, dart-
ing, possessive touches;
the bellboy's conspiracy,
distaste of the outraged.

That always strange moment
when the clothes peel away
(bark from an unknown tree)
with, not a blessing moon,
but a city's panelled skyline;
an early warning system

Before, disentangling,
through rain's soft swish,
the muted horns of taxis,
whirl of police or fire engine,
habitual sounds of loneliness
resume the mind again.

WORKING DREAM

At the end of a manuscript
I was studying, a secret message.
A star, a honeycomb, a seashell,
The stately glory of a peacock's tail
Spiralled colour across the page
To end with a space between a lean I
And a warm and open-armed You.

An hour later, you were at the door;
I learnt the word that space was for.

TALISMAN

After talking together
we move, as by a natural
progress, to make love.
Slant afternoon light

on the bed, the unlatched
window, scattered sheets
are part of a pattern
hastening towards memory

as you give yourself
to me with a cry of
joy, not hunger, while
I receive the gift

in ease, not raw desire
& all the superstructure
of the city outside –
twenty iron floors

of hotel dropping
to where the late sun
strikes the shield of
the lake, its chill towers –

are elements in a slowly
developing dream, a talisman
of calm, to invoke against
unease, to invoke against harm.

THAT ROOM

Side by side on the narrow bed
We lay, like chained giants,
Tasting each other's tears, in terror
Of the news which left little to hide
But our two faces that stared
To ritual masks, absurd and flayed.

Rarely in a lifetime comes such news
Shafting knowledge straight to the heart
Making shameless sorrow start –
Not childish tears, querulously vain –
But adult tears that hurt and harm,
Seeping like acid to the bone.

Sound of hooves on the midnight road
Raised a dramatic image to mind:
The Dean riding late to Marley?
But we must suffer the facts of self;
No one endures a similar fate
And no one will ever know

What happened in that room
But when we came to leave
We scrubbed each other's tears
Prepared the usual show. That day
Love's claims made chains of time and place
To bind us together more: equal in adversity.

TIDES

The window blown
open, that summer
night, a full moon

occupying the sky
with a pressure of
underwater light

a pale radiance
glossing the titles
behind your head

& the rectangle
of the bed where,
after long separation,

we begin to make
love quietly, bodies
turning like fish

in obedience to
the pull & tug
of your great tides.

CAVE

The rifled honeycomb
of the high-rise hotel
where a wind tunnel moans.
While jungleclad troops
ransack the Falls, race
through huddled streets,
we lie awake, the wide
window washed with rain,
your oval face, and tide
of yellow hair luminous
as you turn to me again
seeking refuge as the
cave of night blooms
with fresh explosions.

TRACKS, I

I

The vast bedroom
a hall of air,
our linked bodies
lying there.

II

As I turn to kiss
your tight black
curls, full breasts,
heat flares from
your unmarked skin
and your eyes widen as
deeper, more certain
and often I enter
to search possession
of where your being
is hidden in flesh:

III

I shall miss you
creaks the mirror
into which the scene
will shortly disappear;
the vast bedroom
a hall of air, the
tracks of our bodies
fading there, while
giggling maids push
a trolley of fresh
linen down the corridor.

THE SCREECH OWL

The night is a great sleeping city
where the wind breathes. It has come
from far to our bed's safety, this June
midnight. You sleep, a hazel tree rustles,
I am led towards the borders of dream.
Comes that cry, nearing, disappearing,
a gleam fleeing through woods, or shades
some might say, which flit through hell.
(Of this midsummer night cry, how much
I might say, and of your eyes.) Though it is
only a bird called the screech owl, calling
from the depths of these suburban woods. And
already our bodies smell of the rankness
of the small hours, as under the warm sun
the bone pierces, while stars fade at street ends.

after Phillipe Jacottet

MATINS

That final bright morning you climb
The stairs to my balcony bed,
Unasked; unashamed: naked.
Barely a please was said
But in the widening light
Our bodies linked, blazed,
Our spirits melded. The dawn
Of a capital city swarmed
Beneath us, but we were absorbed,
Your long hair tenting your head,
Your body taut as a divining rod.
There is in such exchanges a harvest,
A source or wellspring of sweetness,
Grace beyond sense, body's intelligence.

PASTORALS

I

'Lyricize this, my fretful love,
Love is a claw within a velvet glove,
Love is a movement of a withered hand,
Love is a dawn illusion
Blandly planned:
How can brief blood understand?'

II

'Love is the movement of the race
Blood-blindfolded to a chosen face:
Movement of unlawful limbs
In a marriage of two whims:
Consummation of disgrace
Beneath the burning-glass of grace.'

III

And yet, my love, we two have come
Into love as to a lighted room
Where all is gaiety and humbling grace.
Hearts long bruised with indolence,
With harsh fatigue of unrelated fact, can trace
Redeeming patterns of experience.

Return

The son of the King of the Moy
met a girl in green woods on mid-summer's day:
she gave him black fruit from thorns
and the full of his arms
of strawberries, where they lay.

HARVEST

That first wild summer
we watched each other,
my graying hair and
wary eyes slowly drawn
to be warmed by your
flaring hair, abundant body.

No ice princess, you call
me down from my high tower –
On our first night together
I awoke, to watch over
your rich shape, a shower
of gold in the moonlight.

And an old fable stirred:
a stag rising from a wet brake,
– Danae deluged by Zeus?
Rather, youth's promise fulfilled,
homely as a harvest field
from my Tyrone childhood

Where I hoist warm sheaves
to tent them into golden stooks,
each detail, as I wade
through the moonlit stubble,
crayon bright, as in
a child's colouring book.

I

They talk of rural innocence but most marriages
Here (or wherever the great middle-
Class morality does not prevail) are arranged
Post factum, products of a warm night,
A scuffle in a ditch, boredom spiced
By curiosity, by casual desire –
That ancient game …
Rarely
That ancient sweetness.

In school
Her hair was unstinted as harvest
Inundating her thin shoulderblades
Almost to her waist. As she ran
The boys called and raced after her
Across the schoolyard, repeating her name
Like something they meant. Until she stopped:
Then they dwindled away, in flight
From a silence.

But after dark
The farmhands flocked to her door
Like migrant starlings, to sit by the fireside
Pretending indifference, or hang around outside
Waiting for a chance to call her away
Down the slope, into darkness.

Finally,
Of course, she gave in. Flattered,
Lacking shrewdness, lacking a language?

II

By the time she was fourteen she was known
As a 'good thing'. By the time she was sixteen
She had to go to England 'to get rid of it'.
By the time she was eighteen, no one 'decent'
Or 'self-respecting' would touch her:
With her tangle of hair and nervously
Darkened eyes, she looked and spoke like
'A backstreets whure'.
                    Condemnation
Never lacks a language!

III

She married, eventually, some casual
Labourer from the same class as herself
For in the countryside even beauty
Cannot climb stairs. But my eye
Still follows an early vision when
Grace inhabited her slight form,
Fragrant as a pine sapling,
Though my hesitant need to praise
Has had to wait a sanction
Greater than sour morality's
                    To see the light of day:
                    For lack of courage
                    Often equals lack of a language
                    And the word of love is
                    Hardest to say.

ABSENCE

One by one, the small boys nod off.
The only light left is my Prefect's torch.
For an hour I have patrolled the dorm,
Checking that Romeo Forte is not snoring,
That Gubby Lenny is not homesick, weeping,
The terrible O'Neill twins not whispering.
Surely Dean Roughan will not do the rounds
Tonight, so I have a chance to warm up again
My letter to a convent girl in Lurgan,
Concealed inside our Modern History volume.
I can still smell the fragrance of your hair,
Your small ears, like seashells, and so on.
The waterpipes knock, the great bells sound.
To the chill dark of my cubicle I summon
The sweet blessing of a girlish presence,
Shaping my lips to kiss her absence.

FAIR HEAD

Night after night
we lay, embracing,
under the shadows
of Sir John's Castle.

Or in the hedge
by the lodge gates
– Maureen Canavan –
arms straining

towards a freedom
neither of us felt
willing to mention:
abhorred temptation!

Hugging and kissing
but holding our lower
parts separate and
rigid as gate posts

leading to adventures
we could never enter
blithely together;
love's untilled estate

in moonlight around us,
from cobwebbed cellars
the mocking laughter
of a ghostly landlord.

Tonguetied I let
you drift away, with
nothing done or said,
only the lost fragrance

of your fair head –
ceannbhán, a bog blossom –
on warm summer evenings
along the Waterside

or bent towards mine
in Glencull choir
as the handbell shivers
O Salutaris Hostia.

ABOVE THE POOL

We were nearly
pressed against each other
on the stairs
(you, one step above
with your mother:
I, one step below
with my aunt)

of the white mosque
of a cinema
in Bundoran, high above
the small hotels, ice-cream
parlours, the Atlantic
working against
Roguey rocks.

And my eyes
were asking yours,
and yours were asking mine
for something more
than a glance on a stair;
the seawrack odour
of Donegal air.

We crossed
on the wooden stairs
above the bathing pool
next day, and you halted
with your sun-warmed hair
expectant eyes, wedge-heeled
wartime shoes

waiting for me
to speak, while hit tunes
from the Majestic ballroom
sobbed in my brain:
I'll close my eyes,
Shine on, Victory Moon,

And I walked on
balancing all my hunger for
that mysterious other
against my need to be alone,
to hug rocks, search blue pools
for starfish, in this
my last summer of loneliness.

VIRGO HIBERNICA

Dare I yet confront
that memory? She poses
on a moist hillside or
stalks through the groin
of the woods on Sunday
mornings, an innocently
accomplished huntress,
acorns snapping beneath
her feet.

Her hair is chestnut
light over the stained
freedom of a raincoat;
each breast kernel-slight
under unbleached wool:
as I trudge docile
by her flank, I feel
the gravitational pull
of love.

And fight back, knowing
gold of her cheekbones,
her honied, naïve speech
drains power from manhood;
yet for years we walk
Enniskerry, Sallygap,
clasped in talk, neither
willing to let the other
come or go ...

RETURN

From the bedroom you can see
straight to the fringe of the woods
with a cross staved gate to re-
enter childhood's world:
                                        the pines
wait, dripping.

                        Crumbling black-
berries, seized from a rack
of rusty leaves, maroon tents
of mushroom, pillars uprooting
with a dusty snap;

                              as the bucket
fills, a bird strikes from the bushes
and the cleats of your rubber boot crush
a yellow snail's shell to a smear
on the grass
                    (while the wind starts
the carrion smell of the dead fox
staked as warning).

Seeing your former
self saunter up the garden path
afterwards, would you flinch,
acknowledging
that sensuality,
that innocence?

Love, A Greeting

Homage

Woman is mortal woman: she abides

GRAVES

LOVE, A GREETING

Love, a greeting
in the night, a
passing kindness,
wet leaf smell
of hair, skin

or a lifetime's
struggle to exchange
with the strange
thing inhabiting
a woman –
                    face,
breasts, buttocks,
the honey sac
of the cunt –

luring us to forget,
beget, a form of truth
or (the last rhyme
tolls its half tone)
an answer to death.

SHEELA NA GIG*

The bloody tentflap opens. We slide
into life, slick with slime and blood.
Cunt, or Cymric *cwm*, Chaucerian *quente*,
the first home from which we are sent
into banishment, to spend our whole life
cruising to return, raising a puny mast
to sail back into those moist lips
that overhang the *labia minora* and *clitoris.*
To sigh and die upon the Mount of Venus,
layer after layer of warm moss,
to return to that first darkness!
Small wonder she grins at us, from gable
or church wall. For the howling babe
life's warm start: man's question mark?

*Literally, Sheela of the Breasts (but more probably of the Thighs), whose vulva is seen on many medieval Irish churches, as warning or fertility symbol. Nobody knows.

MESSAGE

With a body
heavy as earth
she begins to speak

her words
are dew, bright
deadly to drink

her hair
the damp mare's
nest of the grass

her arms,
thighs, chance
of a swaying branch

her secret
message, shaped
by a wandering wind

puts the eye
of reason out;
so novice, blind,

ease your
hand into the
rot smelling crotch

of a hollow
tree, and find
two pebbles of quartz

protected by
a spider's web:
her sunless breasts.

SESKILGREEN

A circle of stones
surviving behind a
guttery farmhouse,

the capstone phallic
in a thistly meadow:
Seskilgreen Passage Grave.

Cup, circle,
triangle beating
their secret dance

(eyes, breasts,
thighs of a still
fragrant goddess).

I came last in May
to find the mound
drowned in bluebells

with a fearless wren
hoarding speckled eggs
within a stony crevice

while cattle
swayed sleepily
under low branches

lashing the ropes
of their tails
across the centuries.

FOR THE HILLMOTHER

Hinge of silence
        creak for us
Rose of darkness
        unfold for us
Wood anemone
        sway for us
Blue harebell
        bend to us
Moist fern
        unfurl for us
Springy moss
        uphold us
Branch of pleasure
        lean on us
Leaves of delight
        murmur for us
Odorous wood
        breathe on us
Evening dews
        pearl for us
Freshet of ease
        flow for us
Secret waterfall
        pour for us
Hidden cleft
        speak to us
Portal of delight
        inflame us
Hill of motherhood
        wait for us
Gate of birth
        open for us

COATLICUE

Your body is small
squat, tawny as
a Nahautl Indian,
an Aztec image
of necessary death:

casually born
of the swirl of
a river, tossed
up by tides –
sexual flotsam –

regard those swart
small breasts that
will never give milk
though around inflamed
nipples, love-bites

multiply like scars.
Salt wind of desire
upon the flesh!
Black hair swings
over your shoulders

as you bear darkness
down toward me, and
across the sun-robed
pyramid, obsidian knives
resume their sacrifice.

MEDUSA

Again she appears,
The putrid fleshed woman
Whose breath is ashes,
Hair a writhing net of snakes!
Her presence strikes gashes
Of light into the skull,
Rears the genitals

Tears away all
I had so carefully built –
Position, marriage, fame –
As heavily she glides towards me
Rehearsing the letters of my name
As if tracing them from
A rain streaked stone.

All night we turn
Towards an unsounded rhythm
Deeper, more fluent than breathing.
In the pale light of morning
Her body relaxes: the hiss of seed
Into that mawlike womb
Is the whimper of death being born.

BEYOND THE LISS*

Sean the hunchback, sadly
Walking the road at evening
Hears an errant music,
Clear, strange, beautiful,

And thrusts his moon face
Over the wet hedge
To spy a ring of noble
Figures dancing, with –

A rose at the centre –
The lustrous princess.

Humbly he pleads to join,
Saying, 'Pardon my ugliness,
Reward my patience,
Heavenly governess.'

Presto! like the frog prince
His hump grows feather
Light, his back splits,
And he steps forth, shining

Into the world of ideal
Movement where (stripped
Of stale selfishness,
Curdled envy) all

**liss*: a fairy mound or fort.

Act not as they are
But might wish to be –
Planets assumed in
A sidereal harmony –

Strawfoot Sean
Limber as any.

But slowly old habits
Reassert themselves, he
Quarrels with pure gift,
Declares the boredom

Of a perfect music,
And, with goatish nastiness,
Seeks first to insult,
Then rape, the elegant princess.

Presto! with a sound
Like a rusty tearing
He finds himself lifted
Again through the air

To land, sprawling,
Outside the hedge,
His satchel hump securely
Back on his back.

Sean the hunchback, sadly
Walking the road at evening

To wake up and discover –
a *splairge* of chill water –
that she was but a forthright woman
on whom we had bestowed
(because of the crook of an elbow,
the swing of a breast or hip,
a glance, half-understood)
divinity or angelhood?

Raised by the fury of our need,
supplicating, lusting, grovelling
before the tall tree of Artemis,
the transfiguring bow of Diana,
the rooting vulva of Circe, or
the slim shape of a nymph,
luring, dancing, beckoning:
all her wild disguises!

And now she does not shine,
or ride, like the full moon,
gleam or glisten like cascades
of uncatchable, blinding water;
disturb, like the owl's cry,
predatory, hovering: marshlight,
moonstone, or devil's daughter,
but conducts herself like any

Ordinary citizen, orderly or slattern,
giving us a piece of her mind,

pacifying or scolding children,
or, more determinedly, driving
or riding to her office, after
depositing the children in a *crêche*,
while she fulfills herself,
'competing with the best.'

Of course, she is probably saying
the same thing of us, as Oisin,
our tall hero from Fairyland,
descends or falls from the saddle
to dwindle into an irritable husband,
worn down by the quotidian,
unwilling to transform the night
with love's necessary shafts of light.

Except that when the old desires stir
– fish under weed-tangled waters –
will she remember that we once were
the strange ones who understood
the powers that coursed so furiously
through her witch blood, prepared
to stand, bareheaded, open handed,
to recognise, worship and obey:

To defy custom, redeem the ordinary,
with trembling heart, and obeisant knee
to kneel, prostrate ourselves again,
if necessary, before the lady?

A fuel fiercer than love; bitterness!

As I bend to this long neglected page
In my stonecold attic, another, younger man
Bends to your brown face: another less
Mottled hand reaches out to cover yours
Which lately lay so warm in mine
Now desperately trying to forge a line
Where furious, calm, I can control my rage,
Wrestle my pain so as to take up again
My old fashioned courtly poet's pilgrimage
Towards the ideal, woman or windmill;
Seething inside, but smiling like a sage.

Tracks

If we pursue beauty, we have always
to follow another face.

MONDOR: *Mallarmé*

MOUNT VENUS

Forever the slim demon
elevates his claret cup
saying, there is but one life,
fill and drink up, while

over the villa'd suburbs
his careless laughter rings
before his snout vanishes
among a lady's earrings.

LA BELLE*

A flourish of silver
trumpets as the royal
favorite is prepared
for the swansdown bed.

Fingers and toes
palpable, succulent
as those pert curves
of mouth, snub nose.

The string of pearls
on her stomach folds
luminously pendent
as rare raindrops

While a pair of pure-
bred hunting hounds
snuffle her plump
and perfumed hands.

A candid light streams
from such guileless &
dimpled nakedness, such
cherubic openness!

And the fillet of
gold she bears so
demurely in honor
of her sovereign master,

*La Belle O'Murphí, a cobbler's daughter from Limerick, who became a royal courtesan, and a favored model of Boucher.

Upon her piled strands
of auburn Irish hair,
looped to reveal her
gold neck collar.

A king's treasure
of roseate flesh
caught on canvas
for a king's pleasure

With a full quiver
of arrows, a dangling
brace of pheasant,
all stamped; royal property.

TURNHOLE

We part the leaves.

Small, squat, naked
Jim Toorish stood in
the churning middle
of the dark turnhole.

Black hair on his poll,
a roll of black hair
over his stomach, that
strange tussock below.

With a rib of black
fur along his back
from thick neckbone
to simian buttocks.

From which – *inescapable* –
his father root sprang,
gross as a truncheon,
normal as a pumphandle.

And cheerfully splashing,
scooping chill waters over
his curls, his shoulders –
that hairy thing!

To cleanse everything
but our prurient giggling
which took long years
for me to exorcise

Until I saw him again,
upright and glorious,
a satyr, laughing in
the spray at Florence.

The infinite softness
& complexity of a body
in repose. The hinge

of the ankle bone de-
fines the flat space
of a foot, its puckered

flesh & almost arch.
The calf's heavy curve
sweeping down against

the bony shin, or up
to the warm bulges &
hollows of the knee

describes a line of
gravity, energy as
from shoulder knob

to knuckle, the arm
cascades, round the
elbow, over the wrist.

The whole body a system
of checks & balances –
those natural shapes

a sculptor celebrates
sea-worn caves, pools,
boulders, tree-trunks –

or, at every hand's turn,
a crop of temptation:
arm & thigh opening

on softer, more secret
areas, hair sprouting
crevices, odorous nooks

& crannies of love,
awaiting the impress
of desire, a fervent

homage, or tempting
to an extinction of
burrowing blindness.

(Deviously uncurling
from the hot clothes
of shame, a desert

father's dream of
sluttish nakedness,
demon with inflamed

breasts, dangling
tresses to drag man
down to hell's gaping

vaginal mouth.)

To see the model
as simply human

a mild housewife
earning pocket money
for husband & child

is to feel the dark
centuries peel away
to the innocence of

the white track on
her shoulders where
above brown flesh

the brassiere lifts
to show the quiet of
unsunned breasts &

to mourn & cherish
each melancholy proof
of mortality's grudge

against perfection:
the appendix scar
lacing the stomach

the pale stitches on
the wailing wall of
the rib-cage where

the heart obediently
pumps.

What homage
is worthy for such

a gentle unveiling?
To nibble her ten
toes, in an ecstacy

of love, to drink
hair, like water?
(Fashion designers

would flatten her
breasts, level the
curves of arse &

stomach, moulding
the mother lode
that pulses beneath

to a uniformity
of robot bliss.)

On cartridge paper

an army of pencils
deploy silently to
lure her into their

net of lines while
from & above her
chilled, cramped

body blossoms
a late flower:
her tired smile.

THE HUNT

Chased beast, exultant huntress,
the same flood of hair.
I gripped you, you seized me.
In the battle, our limbs tangle forever.

But already impatient dawn breaks.

Blithe, surprised,
we refind our bodies.
So far, there is only someone else.

after André Frénaud

THE QUEEN OF SHEBA

The Queen of Sheba wears a green diadem.
Is it for love, shame, or loving shame?
It's one of the marvels she owned
When she died to an angel's trumpet,
A blast of wind.

*

She grants me an ecstatic smile
She gives me kisses, strange and false,
She swims among my animals, the watching fish
She makes airy flights with her limbs.

Long legs & hair. This woman is a born diver,
More imperceptibly than nature she settles like a rose
At the bottom of the sea's garden.

*

A twirl on her rose stockings
An embroidered belt red at her waist
Provocative, she waits

Lean and naked a second
After rolling small tight
Pants slowly down her thighs

Breasts, two swarthy pears,
Shoulders sloping to magnificent arms,
But, better than all, her stomach

Pit proferring an enormous tuft,
Pungent and black, like a sin
Only admiration can crush.

*

The feminine fur lies lower still.
Lord you have seen my guilty eye
Slither there. So the jungle bird
Falls to the alligator, its laughing jaws.
The dreaming tropics, its streams, the ripeness
Of paradise, music's primal themes.

*

Begin at the pool's bottom
Where words thicken, obscene and cold.

Shudder of the horse of death!
He submits to the temptation of the black mouth
Hidden beneath the enamelled face,
The game of curtains, tangled legs, embrace.

*

It's true I have never, never prayed
Said the tall lady with the slim waist
But let him have my breasts, my belly, my youth
And see if he isn't satisfied.

*

She sucks, kisses, wears out and awakes.
When I am finally broken, she flies off,
Blowing my precious memories out –
A trail of blue bubbles.

How much man suspects the mouth he adores
But there was ecstasy there that he still pursues
And vitality. He longs for the smell,
The taste, the colour of women's bodies,
Their flexibility, their faithlessness,
Chaste death smiling through their nacreous limbs
And afterwards that sadness
Which he knows full well.

after Pierre Jean Jouve

CAUGHT

A slight girl and easily got rid of:
He took his pleasure in an idle dance,
Laughed to hear her cry under him,
But woke to find his body in a trance.
Wherever he walked, he seemed to see
Her approaching figure, whoever spoke
He strained for echoes of her voice,
And, in a rage of loss, turned back
To where she slept, hands clasped on
Small breasts in a posture of defence.
Conqueror turned plaintiff, he tries
To uncurl them, to see long-lashed eyes
Turn slowly up, hear a meek voice say:
'Are you back, my love, back to stay?'

SNOWFIELD

The paleness of your flesh.

Long afterwards, I gaze happily
At my warm tracks radiating

Across that white expanse.

TRACKS, II

I

The vast bedroom
a hall of air,
our linked bodies
lying there.

II

As I turn to kiss
your long, black
hair, small breasts,
heat flares from
your fragrant skin,
your eyes widen as
deeper, more certain
and often, I enter
to search possession
of where your being
hides in flesh.

III

Behind our eyelids
a landscape opens,
a violet horizon
pilgrims labour across,
a sky of colours
that change, explode

a fantail of stars,
the mental lightning
of sex illuminating
the walls of the skull;
a floating pleasure dome.

IV

I shall miss you
creaks the mirror
into which the scene
shortly disappears:
the vast bedroom
a hall of air, the
tracks of our bodies
fading there, while
giggling maids push
a trolley of fresh
linen down the corridor.

THE HUNTSMAN'S APOLOGY

You think I am brutal and without pity but at least I execute cleanly because, like any true killer, I wish to spare the victim. There are worse deaths. I have seen the wounded bird trail her wing, and attract only the scavenger. 'Help me' he croaks as he hops near. One dart of her beak would settle him, for he is only a pale disciple of Death, whom he follows at a distance. But she needs sympathy and when he calls 'I am more unhappy than you' her womanly heart revives and she takes him under her broken wing. Her eyesight is poor and her senses dulled but she feels an echo of lost happiness as he stirs against her breast. She does not realise that he is quietly settling down to his favourite meal of dying flesh, happily enveloped in the smell of incipient putrefaction. The pain grows and spreads through her entire body until she cries aloud but it is too late to shake off his implanted beak. He grinds contentedly on and, as she falls aside, his head shoots up, like a scaldy out of a nest. His eye is alert, his veins coursing with another's blood, and for a brief moment, as he steps across the plain without looking back, his tread is firm as a conqueror's.

LITANY

Conch, crack, snatch or tender part,
Hole, lovelane, star above the garter,
Cunt, cunny, *cwithe* (O.E.) or twat,
cavity, burrow, and honey harbour.
Cockpit, cocklane, or blind alley,
for the welsh, *cwm*, cleft or valley,
of if the going's good: love's highway,
tantrics sliding through the yoni!
Such litanies of homage and horror,
To meet our fate, that mysterious other,
Navis, a vessel for the long voyage home,
Egyptian K-a-t being also Mother.

Ladies I have lain
            with in darkened rooms
sweet shudder of flesh
            behind shadowy blinds
long bars of light
            across tipped breasts
warm mounds of
            breathing sweetness
young flesh redolent
            of crumpled roses
the tender anxiety
            of the middle-aged
a hovering candle
            hiding blue veins.
eloquent exhaustion
            watching light fade
as your drowsy partner
            drifts towards the
warm shores of sleep
            and you slowly awake
to confront again
            the alluring lie
of searching through
            another's pliant body
for something missing
            in your separate self
while profound night
            like a black swan
goes pluming past.

CUCHULAIN
(to his charioteer):
Look, Loig, behind –
civil, sensible women are listening,
grey daggers in their right hands,
gold plate on their breasts.
A fine figure they cut,
fierce as warriors in their chariots:
clearly, my wife has changed!

(to his mistress):
Show no fear and she will not approach.
Come, sit beside me
in the sun-warmed prow
of my great chariot
and I will protect you from
all the female hordes of Ulster.
Though the daughter of Forgall come
storming with her company of women
she will not dare lay a hand on me.

(to Emer his wife):
I shun you, woman,
as all creatures shun the yoke.
That stiff spear in your trembling hand,
your thin, lean knife,
cannot harm my majesty,
far above a woman's strength.

EMER:

A question, fickle though you are,
Cuchulain. Why did you shame me
before all the women of Ulster,
the women of Ireland, and
all mannerly people?
I came, under your care,
the full strength of your bond,
and though success makes you vain,
it may be a while, little hound,
before you get rid of me.

CUCHULAIN:

A question, Emer,
Why would you not let
me linger with a woman?
To begin with, this girl
is chaste, sincere, and clever,
fit to be the consort of a king,
conquering across heavy seas.
Style, grace and breeding,
embroidery, husbandry and weaving,
thrift, common sense and character,
all these she has, as well as herds
of horses and cattle.
There is little she would
not do for her lover's wife
if it were agreed between them.
Ah, Emer, you will never find

a good-looking, death-dealing,
triumphant champion like I am!

EMER:
And maybe the woman you follow is no better.
But everything glittering is beautiful,
everything new is bright, everything far is fair,
everything lacking is lovely, everything
    customary is sour,
everything familiar is neglected,
until all knowledge be known.

after the early Irish

Discords

Picnic

Your *mistake*, my *mistake.*
Small heads writhing,
a basket of snakes.

UPROOTING

My love, while we talked
They removed the roof. Then
They started on the walls,
Panes of glass uprooting
From timber, like teeth.
But you spoke calmly on,
Your example of courtesy
Compelling me to reply.
When we reached the last
Syllable, nearly accepting
Our positions, I saw that
The floorboards were gone:
It was clay we stood upon.

IN THE DARK

As the thunderstorm
hovers over the car

your hand roves
over me, a frantic claw,

your mouth clamps
upon mine.

To kiss, in hunger
to kiss, in friendliness

not this salt
smart of anger and despair

an acrid salutation
bruising the lips.

After, in the dark
a voice in anger

by the roadside
a worn car tyre

smouldering, a stench
of burning rubber.

DISCORDS

I

There is a white light in the room.
It is anger. He is angry, or
She is angry, or both are angry.
To them it is absolute, total,
It is everything; but to the visitor,
The onlooker, the outsider,
It is the usual, the absurd;
For if they did not love each other
Why should they heed a single word?

II

Another sad goodbye at the airport;
Neither has much to say, *en garde*,
Lest a chance word turn barbed.
You bring me, collect me, each journey
Not winged as love, but heavy as duty;
Lohengrin's swan dipping to Charon's ferry.

III

A last embrace at the door,
Your lovely face made ugly
By a sudden flush of tears
Which tell me more than any phrase,
Tell me what I most need to hear,
Wash away and cleanse my fears:
You have never ceased to love me.

I

Amo, ergo sum

I hold your ash pale
Face in the hollow
Of my hand and warm
It slowly back to life.
As the eyelashes stir
Exposing brown flecked
Pupils, soft with
Belief in my existence,
I make a transference
Of trust, and know
The power of the magician:
My palm begins to glow.

II

The Blow

Anger subsiding, I could
Still see the fiery mark
Of my fingers dwindle
On your cheek, but
Did not rush to kiss
The spot. Hypocrisy
Is not love's agent,
Though our fierce awareness
Would distort instinct
To stage a mood.

III

Pitch-Dark

Truths we upturn
Too near the bone;
Shudder of angels
Into grimacing stone:
Whatever hope we
Woke with, gone.
We cannot imagine
A further dawn.
Only the will says –
Soldier on!

SUMMER STORM

I

A Door Banging

Downstairs, a door
banging, like a
blow upon sleep

pain bleeding away
in gouts of accusation
& counter accusation;

heart's release
of bitter speech.

II

Mosquito-Hunt

Heat contracts the
walls, smeared with
the bodies of insects

we crush, absurd-
ly balanced upon
the bedsprings

twin shadows on
the wall rising
& falling as

we swoop &
quarrel, like
wide winged bats.

ABOVE

Love transfixes me
with an accusing eye

– I have been angry
with you, all day,

ever since, clumsy,
suspicious, heavy-

footed, you recalled
the terms of our bargain

neither to put a halter
on either, bridle or bit.

But no sooner, my dear,
were you free of my arms,

dismounted, like any mortal,
from saddle and pommel,

than you renege, insist
on speaking anxiously

of houses, properties,
mortgages, marriages,

all that grid of society
we had glimpsed so gloriously

from above, but which again
seems to you necessary

as we float down to it.

THE GOLDEN HOOK

Two fish float:

one slowly downstream
into the warm
currents of the known

the other tugging
against the stream,
disconsolate twin,

the golden
marriage hook
tearing its throat.

TEARING

I

I sing your pain
as best I can
   seek
like a gentle man
   to assume
the proffered blame.

But the pose breaks.
The sour facts remain.
   It takes
two to make or break
   a marriage.
Unhood the falcon!

II
Pastourelle

Hands on the pommel
long dress trailing
over polished leather
riding boots, a spur
jutting from the heel,
& beneath, the bridle path,
strewn with rusty apples,
brown knobs of chestnut,
meadow saffron and acorn.

Then we were in the high
ribbed dark of the trees
where animals move stealth-
ily, coupling & killing,
while we talked nostalgically
of our lives, bedevilled
& betrayed by lost love –
the furious mole, tunnelling
near us his tiny kingdom –

& how slowly we had come
to where we wished each other
happiness, far and apart, as
a hawk circled the wood,
& a victim cried, the sound
of hooves rising & falling
upon bramble & fern, while
a thin growth of rain gather-
ed about us, like a cowl.

III
Never

In the gathering dark
I caress your head
as you thrash out
flat words of pain:
'There is no way back,
I can feel it happening;
we shall never be
what we were, again.'

Never, a solemn bell
tolling through
that darkened room
where I cradle your head,
only a glimmer left
in the high window
over what was once
our marriage bed.

Rue Daguerre, how we searched
til we found it! Beyond
the blunt pawed lion of Denfert
to where, after the bustle
of an open stalled market
you halt, before stooping
into a cobbled courtyard.

Symbol of the good life
this silence, each bend-
ing to his chosen task;
a Japanese framer, tire-
less and polite, tending
a grafted cherry tree as
if it were his exiled self

which foamed to brief
and splendid blossom
each European spring.
The florist who made a
speciality of wreaths,
flower woven cartwheels
a cortège on his walls

smothered at Christmas
by fragrant limbs of fir.
The old woman stitching
moleskin sacks and bags
while her gross, gelded
cat dozed towards death
along its sunlit bench.

On Sunday mornings,
white canes racked,
two blind men played
the accordion, those
simple rippling tunes
that tore the heart;
sous les toits de Paris.

Or, *la vie en rose*,
setting for a shared
life, slowly broken,
wrenched, torn apart,
change driving its
blunt wedge through
what seemed permanent:

the cobbles uprooted,
the framer beheaded
in a multiple accident,
a giant tower hulking
over the old market,
the traffic's roar
(waves grinding near

a littered shore)
while time whirls
faster and faster,
j'attendrai tous
les jours, a blind
accordion playing
to a funeral wreath.

NO MUSIC

I'll tell you a sore truth, little understood
It's harder to leave, than to be left:
To stay, to leave, both sting wrong.

You will always have me to blame,
Can dream we might have sailed on;
From absence's rib, a warm fiction.

To tear up old love by the roots,
To trample on past affections:
There is no music for so harsh a song.

The spider's web
of your handwriting
on a blue envelope

brings up too much
to bear, old sea-sick-
ness of love, retch

of sentiment, night
& day devoured by
the worm of delight

which turns to
feed upon itself;
emotion running so

wildly to seed
between us until
it assumes a third

a ghost or child's
face, the soft skull
pale as an eggshell

& the life-cord
of the emerging body –
fish, reptile, bird –

which trails
like the cable
of an astronaut

as we whirl & turn
in our bubble of
blood & sperm

before the gravities
of earth claim us
from limitless space.

*

Now, light years later
your nostalgic letter
admitting failure,

claiming forgiveness.
When fire pales to
so faint an ash

so frail a design
why measure guilt
your fault or mine:

but blood seeps where
I sign before tearing
down the perforated line.

HERBERT STREET REVISITED

I

A light is burning late
in this Georgian Dublin street:
someone is leading our old lives!

And our black cat scampers again
through the wet grass of the convent garden
upon his masculine errands.

The pubs shut: a released bull,
Behan shoulders up the street,
topples into our basement, roaring 'John!'

A pony and donkey cropped flank
by flank under the trees opposite;
short neck up, long neck down,

as Nurse Mullen knelt by her bedside
to pray for her lost Mayo hills,
the bruised bodies of Easter Volunteers.

Animals, neighbours, treading the pattern
of one time and place into history,
like our early marriage, while

tall windows looked down upon us
from walls flushed light pink or salmon
watching and enduring succession.

II

As I leave, you whisper,
'don't betray our truth'
and like a ghost dancer,
invoking a lost tribal strength
I halt in tree-fed darkness

to summon back our past
and celebrate a love that eased
so kindly, the dying bone,
enabling the spirit to sing
of old happiness, when alone.

III

So put the leaves back on the tree,
put the tree back in the ground,
let Brendan trundle his corpse down
the street singing, like Molly Malone.

Let the black cat, tiny emissary
of our happiness, streak again
through the darkness, to fall soft
clawed into a landlord's dustbin.

Let Nurse Mullen take the last
train to Westport, and die upright
in her chair, facing a window
warm with the blue slopes of Nephin.

And let the pony and donkey come –
look, someone has left the gate open –
like hobbyhorses linked in
the slow motion of a dream

parading side by side, down
the length of Herbert Street,
rising and falling, lifting
their hooves through the moonlight.

THE FIRST LAWCASE

According to Leabhar Gabhála, the second invasion of Ireland, after the Flood, was by Partholan, whose wife's behaviour anticipates the freedom of the Brehon Laws.

Partholan went out one day
To tour his wide spread lands;
Leaving his wife and servant,
Both bound by his commands.

Long they waited in his house,
Until the lady, feeling desperate –
A state before unheard of –
Propositioned the pure servant.

Rightly he ignored her,
Stubborn against temptation,
Until she removed her clothes:
Strange work for a decent woman!

Then, so frail is humanity,
Long limbed Topa rose,
And joined the lovely Delgnat,
Lonely upon her couch.

Wise Partholan possessed
A vat of ale, cool and sweet,
From which none might drink
Save through a golden spigot.

Thirsty after their actions,
Topa and Delgnat, truth to tell,
Leapt from bed so urgently
Their mouths met on the barrel.

When Partholan returned
From wandering his wide fields
A surly black demon revealed
The stains on the golden tube.

"Look, the track of the mouth
Of Topa, as low down as this,
And beside it the smear left
By married Delgnat's kiss!"

Whereupon his wife replied:
"Surely the right to complain
Is mine, innocently left
To confront another man.

Honey with a woman, milk with a cat,
A sharp tool with a craftsman,
Goods with a child or spendthrift:
Never couple things like that.

The woman will eat the honey,
The cat lap the new milk,
While the child destroys the things
Not bestowed by the spendthrift.

The craftsman will use the tool,
Because one and one make two:
So never leave your belongings
Long unguarded, without you."

That is the first adultery
To be heard of in Ireland.
Likewise the first lawcase:
The Right of his Wife against Partholan.

after the early Irish

THE POINT

Rocks jagged in morning mist.
At intervals, the foghorn sounds
From the white lighthouse rock
Lonely as cow mourning her calf,
Groaning, belly deep, desperate.

I assisted at such failure once;
A night-long fight to save a calf
Born finally, with broken neck,
It flailed briefly on the straw,
A wide-eyed mother straddling it.

Listen carefully. This is different.
It sounds to guide, not lament.
When the defining light is powerless,
Ships hesitating down the strait
Hear its harsh voice as friendliness.

Upstairs my wife & daughter sleep.
Our two lives have separated now.
But I would send my voice to yours
Cutting through the shrouding mist
Like some friendly signal in distress.

The fog is lifting, slowly.
Flag high, a new ship is entering.
The opposite shore unveils itself,
Bright in detail as a painting,
Alone, but equal to the morning.

Stoney Plain, Honey Field

The old Irish paradise is called
The Land of women, not the Stoney
Plain. And there you can achieve
enlightenment by a discipline
called AN CÁM DILÍS,
the Sweet Way of love.

OBSESSION

Once again, the naked girl
Dances on the lawn
Under the alder trees
Smelling of rain
And ringed Saturn leans
His vast ear over the world:

But though everywhere the unseen
(Scurry of feet, scrape of flint)
Are gathering, I cannot
Protest. My tongue
Lies curled in my mouth –
My power of speech is gone.

Thrash of an axle in snow!
Not until the adept faun-
Headed brother approves
Us both from the darkness
Can my functions return.
Like clockwork, I strike and go.

CLOSED CIRCUIT

An ache, anger
thunder of a hurtling
waterfall in the ears:
in abrupt detail he sees
the room where she lays
her warm, soft body
under another's

her petal mouth
raised to absorb
his probing kiss
and hears her small voice
cry animal cries
in the hissing anguish
the release of

my sweet one
my darling, my love
until they fall apart
(Oh, the merciless track
of jealousy's film)
in a wet calm
like flowers after rain.

A CHARM

When you step near
I feel the dark hood
Descend, a shadow
Upon my mind.

One thing to do,
Describe a circle
Around, about me,
Over, against you:

The hood is still there
But my pupils burn
Through the harsh folds.
You may return

Only as I wish.
But how my talons
Ache for the knob
Of your wrist!

PREMONITION

I

The darkness comes slowly alight.
That flow of red hair I recognise
Over the knob of the shoulder
Down your pale, freckled skin,
The breasts I have never seen;
But slowly the line of the tresses
Begins to stir, a movement

That is not hair, but blood
Flowing. Someone is cutting
Your naked body up:
Strapped in dream helplessness
I hear each thrust of the knife
Till that rising, descending blade
Seems the final meaning of life.

Mutely, you writhe and turn
In tremors of ghostly pain,
But I am lost to intervene,
Blood, like a scarlet curtain,
Swinging across the brain
Till the light switches off –
And silence is darkness again.

II

On the butcher's block
Of the operating theatre
You open your eyes.
Far away, I fall back
Towards sleep, the Liffey
Begins to rise, and knock
Against the quay walls

The gulls curve and scream
Over the Four Courts, over
This ancient creaking house
Where, released from dream,
I lie in a narrow room;
Low-ceilinged as a coffin
The dawn prises open.

CROSSING

Your lithe and golden body
haunts me, as I haunt you:
corsairs with different freights
who may only cross by chance
    on lucky nights.

So our moorings differ.
but scents of your pleasure
still linger disturbingly
around me: fair winds or
    squalls of danger?

There is a way of forgetting you.
But I have forgotten it:
prepared wildly to cut free,
to lurch, like a young man,
    towards ecstasy!

Nightly your golden body turns
& turns in my shuddering dream.
Why is the heart never still,
yielding again to the cardinal
    lure of the beautiful?

Age should bring its wisdom
but in your fragrant presence
my truths are one, swirling
to a litany – sweet privateer –
    of grateful adulation.

THE WOOING OF ETAIN

Fair lady, will you travel
to the marvellous land of stars?
Pale as snow the body there,
Under a primrose crown of hair.

No one speaks of property
In that glittering community:
White teeth shining, eyebrows black,
the foxglove hue on every cheek.

The landscape bright and speckled
As a wild bird's eggs –
However fair Ireland's Plain,
It is sad after the Great Plain!

If the drink is strong in Ireland,
It is stronger in the Honey Field.
I speak of an eternal land
Where the young never die.

Warm, sweet streams water the earth,
And after the choicest of wine and mead,
Those fine and flawless people
Without sin, without guilt, couple.

We can see everyone
without being seen ourselves:
It is the cloud of Adam's transgression
Conceals us from mortal reckoning.

O woman if you join our strong clan,
Your head will sport a golden crown.
Fresh killed pork, new milk and beer,
We shall share, O Lady Fair!

after the early Irish

THE FIRST INVASION OF IRELAND

According to Leabhar Gabhála, the Book of Conquests, the first invasion of Ireland was by relatives of Noah, just before the Flood. Refused entry into the Ark, they consulted an idol which told them to flee to Ireland.

Fleeing from threatened flood, they sailed,
Seeking the fair island, without serpent or claw;
From the deck of their hasty raft watched
The soft edge of Ireland nearward draw.

A sweet confluence of waters, a trinity of rivers,
Was their first resting place:
They unloaded the women and the sensual idol,
Guiding image of their disgrace.

Division of damsels they did there,
The slender, the tender, the dimpled, the round,
It was the first just bargain in Ireland,
There was enough to go round.

Lightly they lay and pleasured
In the green grass of that guileless place:
Ladhra was the first to die;
He perished of an embrace.

Bith was buried in a stone heap,
Riot of mind, all passion spent.
Fintan fled from the ferocious women
Lest he, too, by love be rent.

Great primitive princes of our line –
They were the first, with stately freedom,
To sleep with women in Ireland:
Soft the eternal bed they lie upon.

On a lonely headland the women assembled,
Chill as worshippers in a nave,
And watched the eastern waters gather
Into a great virile flooding wave.

after the early Irish

THE SIEGE OF MULLINGAR, 1963

At the Fleadh Cheoil* in Mullingar
There were two sounds, the breaking
Of glass, and the background pulse
Of music. Young girls roamed
The streets with eager faces,
Shoving for men. Bottles in
Hand, they rowed out a song:
Puritan Ireland's dead and gone,
A myth of O'Connor and O'Faolain.

In the early morning the lovers
Lay on both sides of the canal
Listening on Sony transistors
to the agony of Pope John.
Yet it didn't seem strange, or blasphemous,
This ground bass of death and
Resurrection, as we strolled along:
Puritan Ireland's dead and gone,
A myth of O'Connor and O'Faolain.

Further on, breasting the wind
Waves of the deserted grain harbour
We saw a pair, a cob and his pen,
Most nobly linked. Everything then
In our casual morning vision
Seemed to flow in one direction,
Line simple as a song:
Puritan Ireland's dead and gone,
A myth of O'Connor and O'Faolain.

*A feast or festival of traditional music.

SENTENCE FOR KONORAK*

Extravagantly your stone gestures
encourage and ease our desires
till the clamour dies: it is not
that man is a bare forked animal,
but that sensuousness is betrayed
by sensuality (a smell of burning flesh);

though here face turns to face,
not ashamed (the word barely exists,
so calm the movement, limpid the smile
above your monstrous actions)
that we are rebuked to learn
how, in the proper atmosphere,

the stealthy five-fingered hand
is less thief than messenger,
as the god bends towards her
whose head already sways towards him,
pliant as a lily, while round them,
in a teeming richness, move

the ripe-thighed temple dancers
in a field of force, a coiling honeycomb
of forms, the golden wheel of love.

*Konorak is a tantric temple in Orissa, India

Allegiances

In Loch Lene
a queen went swimming;
a redgold salmon
flowed into her
at full of evening.

after the FÉLIRE OENGUS

IRISH STREET SCENE, WITH LOVERS

A rainy quiet evening, with leaves that hang
Like squares of silk from dripping branches.
An avenue of laurel, and the guttering cry
Of a robin that balances a moment,
Starts and is gone
On some furtive errand of its own.

A quiet evening, with skies washed and grey;
A tiredness as though the day
Swayed towards sleep,
Except for the reserved statement
Of rain on the stone-grey pavement —
Dripping, they move through this marine light,

Seeming to swim more than walk,
Linked under the black arch of an umbrella,
With its assembly of spokes like points of stars,
A globule of water slowly forming on each.
The world shrinks to the soaked, worn
Shield of cloth they parade beneath.

As I walked out at Merval with my wife
Both of us sad, for a private reason,
We found the perfect silence for it,
A beech leaf severed, like the last
Living thing in the world, to crease
The terraced snow, as we
Walked out by Merval.

And the long staged melancholy of allées,
Tree succeeding tree, each glazed trunk
Not a single heaven-invoking nakedness
But a clause, a cold commentary
Of branches, gathering to the stripped
Dignity of a sentence, as we
Walked out by Merval.

There is a sad formality in the Gallic dance,
Linking a clumsy calligraphy of footsteps
With imagined princes, absorbing sorrow
In a larger ritual, a lengthening avenue
Of perspectives, the ice-gripped pond
Our only Hall of Mirrors, as we
Walk back from Merval.

ALL LEGENDARY OBSTACLES

All legendary obstacles lay between
Us, the long imaginary plain,
The monstrous ruck of mountains
And, swinging across the night,
Flooding the Sacramento, San Joaquin,
The hissing drift of winter rain.

All day I waited, shifting
Nervously from station to bar
As I saw another train sail
By, the San Francisco Chief or
Golden Gate, water dripping
From great flanged wheels.

At midnight you came, pale
above the negro porter's lamp.
I was too blind with rain
And doubt to speak, but
Reached from the platform
Until our chilled hands met.

You had been travelling for days
With an old lady, who marked
A neat circle on the grass
With her glove, to watch us
Move into the wet darkness
Kissing, still unable to speak.

WALKING LATE

Walking late
we share night sounds
so delicate the heart misses
a beat to hear them:

shapes in the half-dark
where the deer feed or
rest, the radar of small
ears & horns still alert
under the glooming boles
of the great oaks
                                        to unfold
their knees from the wet grass
with a single thrust & leap away
stiff-legged, in short, jagged
bursts as we approach
                                                  stars lining
our path through the woods
with a low coiling mist
over the nocturnal meadows
so that we seem to wade
through the filaments
of a giant silver web
the brain crevices of a cloud.

*

Bleached and white
as a fish's belly,
a road curves towards the city
which, with the warming dawn,

will surge towards activity again,
the bubble of the Four Courts
overruling the stagnant quays,
their ghostly Viking prows,

and the echoing archways,
tenebrous walls of the Liberties
where we briefly share a life
to which we must return

as we circle uncertainly
towards a home, your
smaller hand in mine,
trustful, still afraid.

THE WATER'S EDGE

Two of your landscapes I take
The long loneliness of Berck Plage
Where you walked, in your plaid uniform,
Directly into the wind.

Or the formal procession
Of horses, under the pale oaks
Of that urban forest where
You first learnt to ride.

There is in love that brief
Jealousy of the other's past
Coming on the charred roots
Of feeling, of ancient grief;

And here, in a third place,
Two of our landscapes seem to join
In a sweet conspiracy of mirrored
Surfaces, to baffle time

As the now heraldic animal
Stands by the water's edge
Lifting its rider against the sky,
A human shield.

LEE SONG

Let me share with you
a glimpse of richness:
two swans startled me
turning low over the Lee,
looking for a nestling place.
I thought of us, our need
for a place to lay our heads;
our flight secret, unheralded.

By the curl and gleam
of water, my sadness
was washed away:
the air was bright
and clear as your forehead,
the linked swans
reached the wood:
my love, come here to stay.

A DREAM OF JULY

Silence
& damp night air
Flowing from the garden
Like a young girl
Dissatisfied with
Her mythic burden
Ceres, corn goddess,
Mistress of summer,
Steps sure-footed over
The sweet smelling
Bundles of grass.
Her abundant body is
Compounded of honey
& gold, the spike
Of each small nipple
A wild strawberry –
Fulfilled in
Spite of herself
She exchanges with
The moon the pale
Gold disc of her face.

ALLEGIANCE

Beyond the village
herds browse peacefully
behind a barred wooden gate,
a warm Constable scene
of swirling shadows & silence;
a river's murmuring presence.

In their cumbrous circle
the huge stones stand,
completing the plain,
attending the dawn,
dew on granite, damp
on a sword blade.

Slowly, in moonlight
I drop to one knee,
solemn as a knight
obeying an ancient precept,
natural as cattle
stooping in river mist.

A FAIR HOUSE

Pleasant the house where
men, women and children
are swayed by the fair
and yellow haired Creide;

with a swift moving groom,
a door-keeper and butler to
carve when the druid sits
among the musicians ...

Berries drip into the bowl
to dye her black shawl.
A crystal vat she has,
pale goblets and glasses.

Lime white, her skin;
quilts line her rushy floor,
silk, her blue cloak,
red gold, her drinking horn.

Her sun room glitters with
yellow gold and silver,
under warm ridged thatch
tufted brown and scarlet.

Two door posts of green
you pass, a shapely hinge,
and the beam of her lintel
far famed for its silver.

More lovely still, her chair,
On the left as you enter,
with a filigree of Alpine gold
about the foot of her bed.

To the right, another bed,
wrought from precious metals,
a hyacinthine canopy,
bronze curtain rods ...

A hundred foot from front
to back is the span
of the house of Creide;
twenty, her noble doorway.

after the early Irish

AFTER A QUARREL

Like a team of horses,
manes lightstreaming,
we race together,
close, and separate.
Another night of sighs
yet our love revives,
a flower in the morning

as timid, uncertain,
you bring me small
conciliatory presents,
which you hold up
in your hands, face
pursed, like a squirrel,
waiting for me to smile.

Honeycomb of reconciliation:
thigh melting into thigh,
mouth into mouth, breast
turning against ribcage:
we make love as though
this small house were
a paradigm of the universe.

WAITING

Another day of dancing summer,
Evelyn kneels on a rock, breasts
Swollen by approaching motherhood,
Hair bleached by the sea winds
To a pale as honey gold, some
Generous natural image of the good.
Sails butterfly to her nakedness,
Surprised to spy through the haze
A curved figure, sleek as a mermaid,
Or bowsprit Venus, of smooth wood,
Courting the sun and not the shade,
Seagulls aureoling her bowed head,
Translucent as Wicklow river gold;
Source of my present guilt and pride.

THE GREAT CLOAK

Smooth and long to swathe
a handsome woman's body,
a shape tall as a bell,
obedient to a fingernail.

Or to encompass her lover
as well, snug as a flea deep
in a featherbed, while their bodies
converse, on a green slope.

Or when the baby is born
to wrap the morsel tenderly
while beasts browse around them
naturally as in Bethlehem.

CHILD

A firefly gleams, then
fades upon your cheek.
Now you hide beneath
everything I write;
love's invisible ink,
heart's watermark.

I want, says Sibylle,
my small daughter,
at the big table.

You don't want
says her lovely mother,
you would like

and, beside, there
is another small
word, missing.

Please, would like
tries the rascal again,
playing it backwards

the silence between
depending on the ruddy
glow of the peach

the size of the plum
small eyes measuring
the pleasures of opposition

against the necessity
to give in. *Please,*
would like, again.

EDGE

Edenlike as your name
this sea's edge garden
where we rest, beneath
the clarity of a lighthouse

To fly into risk,
attempt the dream,
cast off, as we have done
requires true luck

who know ourselves
blessed to have found
between this harbour's arms
a sheltering home

where the vast
tides of the Atlantic
lift to caress
rose coloured rocks.

So fate relents.
Hushed and calm,
safe and secret,
on the edge is best.

She Speaks

Love

My love is no short year's sentence.
It is a grief lodged under the skin,
Strength pushed beyond its bounds –
The four quarters of the world,
The highest point of heaven.
        It is
  A heart breaking or
  Battle with a ghost,
  Striving under water,
  Outrunning the sky or
  Courting an echo.
So is my love, my passion and my devotion
  To him to whom I give them.

after the early Irish

She sings a little
Off-key, for her
Coaxing lover
Who soothes her
To remember when
A huge figure –
The shadow of
Her father, fell
Across her crib,
Harshly shouting,
Startling the rattle
In her throat, and
When the bough
Breaks, she falls
Again, to feel
A different arm
Holding her up,
Safe and sound,
Above the void,
On the tree-top.

I
Reckless

I don't spread out to please
despite what I pretend.
It's to give myself ease,
escaping from the beasts
by surrendering myself.

It matters little with whom.
It's for myself I lie down,
to keep out the night
by drawing it in.

It's to race breathless.
To find a nest
and lose myself.

The death which never tells,
the constant death which fills
me, so far miscarrying,
soon will have its place.

II

Without Pity

To learn about the world,
to discover the one I was deprived of,
I opened my legs.

Large enough not to miss him,
smaller than an eye on a peacock's tail.

Beauty wavers with me,
always defeated huntress.

I am ready, if you please me,
paying in kind, I lose myself.
Instead of passion, curiosity.
Shrewd, I keep my heart in reserve.

And it's always the same dismay.
A hundred bodies, a hundred too many
reveal the weakness of my hope.

All my branches are lopped.
Have I any regrets left?
After so many false caresses
my fine thighs are dead wood.

III

If I Give Myself

Little pleasure, lasting guilt.
I will try all those irrelevant bodies.
If remorse could feed me
I would grow plump.

I no longer know what hurts,
or if I have fear, or hope
to flee their coarse dreams,
flung at me, like beasts.
I tremble when I am brave.
I am sly when I tell the truth.
I sparkle without pleasure.
I am secretive without a secret.
I'm arid as a desert.

I yield, therefore I am.
I care little for their needs.
For a second I free myself,
I exist in spite of all.
I am so proud in the bed,
Radiating, spreadeagled.

My outflung arms shall avenge me,
against my father, against a world
where the sun does not light,
against the rocking moon,
against all the cold that comes.

after André Frénaud

Snow curls in on the cold wind.

Slowly, I push back the door.
After long absence, old habits
Are painfully revived, those disciplines
Which enable us to survive,
To keep a minimal fury alive
While flake by faltering flake

Snow curls in on the cold wind.

Along the courtyard, the boss
Of each cobblestone is rimmed
In white, with winter's weight
Pressing, like a silver shield,
On all the small plots of earth,
Inert in their living death as

Snow curls in on the cold wind.

Seized in a giant fist of frost,
The grounded planes at London Airport,
Mallarmé swans, trapped in ice.
The friend whom I have just left
Will be dead, a year from now
Through her own fault, while

Snow curls in on the cold wind.

Or smothered by some glacial truth?
Thirty years ago, I learnt to reach
Across the rusting hoops of steel
That bound our greening waterbarrel
To save the living water beneath
The hardening crust of ice, before

Snow curls in on the cold wind.

But despair has a deeper crust.
In all our hours together, I never
Managed to ease the single hurt
That edged her towards her death;
Never reached through her loneliness
To save a trust, chilled after

Snow curls in on the cold wind.

I plunged through snowdrifts once,
Above our home, to carry
A telegram to a mountain farm.
Fearful but inviting, they waved me
To warm myself at the flaring
Hearth before I faced again where

Snow curls in on the cold wind.

The news I brought was sadness.
In a far city, someone of their name
Lay dying. The tracks of foxes,
Wild birds as I climbed down
Seemed to form a secret writing
Minute and frail as life when

Snow curls in on the cold wind.

Sometimes, I know that message.
There is a disease called snow-sickness;
The glare from the bright god,
The earth's reply. As if that
Ceaseless, glittering light was
All the truth we'd left after

Snow curls in on the cold wind.

So, before dawn, comfort fails.
I imagine her end, in some sad
Bedsitting room, the steady hiss
Of the gas more welcome than an
Act of friendship, the protective
Oblivion of a lover's caress if

Snow curls in on the cold wind.

In the canyon of the street
The dark snowclouds hesitate,
Turning to slush almost before
They cross the taut canvas of
The street stall, the bustle
Of a sweeper's brush after

Snow curls in on the cold wind.

The walls are spectral, white.
All the trees black-ribbed, bare.
Only veins of ivy, the sturdy
Laurel with its waxen leaves,
Its scant red berries, survive
To form a winter wreath as

Snow curls in on the cold wind.

⁂

What solace but endurance, kindness?
Against her choice, I still affirm
That nothing dies, that even from
Such bitter failure memory grows;
The snowflake's structure, fragile
But intricate as the rose when

Snow curls in on the cold wind.

LÍADAN LAMENTS CUIRITHIR

Joyless
what I have done;
to torment my darling one.

But for fear
of the Lord of Heaven
he would lie with me here.

Not vain,
it seemed, our choice,
to seek Paradise through pain.

I am Líadan,
I loved Cuirithir
as truly as they say.

The short time
I passed with him
how sweet his company!

Forest trees
sighed music for us;
and the flaring blue of seas.

What folly
to turn him against me
whom I had treated most gently!

No whim
or scruple of mine
should have come between

Us, for above
all others, without shame
I declare him my heart's love.

A roaring flame
has consumed my heart:
I will not live without him.

after the early Irish

THE WOUNDED LASS AND THE ELDER

Confidential, she lies to the complaisant ear.
Confidential, she murmurs her first wound,
youth breached like a black castle.
The elder leans tenderly over her tears.
He can staunch nothing, lacking power.
Plaintively, he understands her, protects.
His goodness is outraged, his heart growing younger
so swiftly, deceiving itself ...
                                                  Only too well
she knows that he loves her, and waits. She ignores him.
Or is he her revenge
                                        (Let go my lips)
desiring, without hope, this merciless child.
Oh, let me alone,
Let me complain, without having to pity you!

after André Frénaud

I
No News

'Dear one, no news from you so long.
I went and came back from the Alps,
I went and came back from the Vosges.
The boy you liked, the forester's son,
Who kept a yellow fox cub in the house
Now has a tame deer, which bumps wildly
Against the furniture, on bony stilts.
More news of shooting in the North.
Did you go to Enniskillen, as you said?
Lying alone at night, I see your body
Like Art O Leary, that elegy you translated,
Lying in a ditch before me, dead.
The cherry tree is alight in the garden.
Come back to our little courtyard,' she said.

II
Alone

Again your lost, hurt voice;
'I hope this never happens you,
I wouldn't wish it upon anyone:
To live and dance in lonely fire,
To lie awake at night, listening
For a step that cannot come.
Of course I gave away the cats.
I found their lovesick cries
More than I could easily bear.
Remember our favourite Siamese?
The moment you entered the yard
He and I would both lift an ear.
Now he is dead, you are gone.
I sleep in the same room, alone.'

SHE DREAMS

Habituée of darkness I have become.
Familiar of the secret feeding grounds
Where terror and dismay ceaselessly hatch,
Black forms curling and uncoiling;
The demons of the night feel like friends.

Something furry brushes along my arm,
A bat or screech owl hurtling by.
I clamber over stained rocks and find
The long gathered contents of our house
Swarming with decay, a filthied nest.

I came to where the eggs lay in the grass.
I watched them for a long time, warming them
With my swollen eyes. One after another
They chipped and scraggy heads appeared;
The embryos of our unborn children.

They turn towards me, croaking 'Mother!'
I gather them up into my apron
But the shape of the house has fallen
And you are asleep by the water's edge:
A wind and wave picked skeleton.

I

I go to say goodbye to Minnie Kearney,
that terrible figure who haunted my childhood
but no longer harsh, a human being
merely, hurt by event.

The cottage,
circled by trees, weathered to admonitory
shapes of desolation by the mountain winds,
straggles into view. The rank thistles
and leathery bracken of untilled fields
stretch behind with – a final outcrop –
the hooped figure by the roadside,
its retinue of dogs

which give tongue
as I approach, with savage, whinging cries
so that she slowly turns, a moving nest
of shawls and rags, to view, to stare
the stranger down.

And I feel again
that ancient awe, the terror of a child
before the great hooked nose, the cheeks
dewlapped with dirt, the staring blue
of the sunken eyes, the mottled claws
clutching a stick

but now hold
and return her gaze, to greet her,
as she greets me, in friendliness.
Memories have wrought reconciliation
between us, we talk in ease at last,
like old friends, lovers almost,
sharing secrets

of neighbours
she quarelled with, who now lie
in Garvaghey graveyard, beyond all hatred;
of my family and hers, how she never married,
though a man came asking in her youth
'You would be loath to leave your own'
she sighs, 'and go among strangers' –
his parish ten miles off.

For sixty years
since she has lived alone, in one place.
Obscurely honoured by such confidences,
I idle by the summer roadside, listening,
while the monologue falters, continues,
rehearsing the small events of her life.
The only true madness is loneliness,
the monotonous voice in the skull
that never stops
because never heard.

II

And there
where the dog rose shines in the hedge
she tells me a story so terrible
that I try to push it away,
my bones melting.

Late at night
a drunk came beating at her door
to break it in, the bolt snapping
from the soft wood, the thin mongrels
rushing to cut, but yelping as
he whirls with his farm boots
to crush their skulls.

In the darkness
they wrestle, two creatures crazed
with loneliness, the smell of the
decaying cottage in his nostrils
like a drug, his body heavy on hers,
the tasteless trunk of a seventy year
old virgin, which he rummages while
she battles for life

bony fingers
reaching desperately to push
against his bull neck. 'I prayed
to the Blessed Virgin herself
for help and after a time
I broke his grip.'

He rolls
to the floor, snores asleep,
while she cowers until dawn
and the dogs' whimpering starts
him awake, to lurch back across
the wet bog.

III

And still
the dog rose shines in the hedge.
Petals beaten wide by rain, it
sways slightly, at the tip of a
slender, tangled, arching branch
which, with her stick, she gathers
into us.

'The wild rose
is the only rose without thorns,'
she says, holding a wet blossom
for a second, in a hand knotted
as the knob of her stick.
'Whenever I see it, I remember
the Holy Mother of God and
all she suffered.'

Briefly
the air is strong with the smell
of that weak flower, offering
its crumbled yellow cup
and pale bleeding lips
fading to white

at the rim
of each bruised and heart-
shaped petal.

SHE WALKS ALONE

In the white city of Evora, absence accosted me.
You were reading in bed, while I walked all night alone.
Were you worried about me, or drifting towards sleep?

I saw the temple of Diana, bone white in the moonlight.
I made a private prayer to her, for strength to continue:
Not since convent days have I prayed so earnestly.

A dog came out of the shadows, brushed against my leg.
He followed me everywhere, pushing his nose into my
hand.
Soon the cats appeared, little scraggly bundles of need.

There were more monuments, vivid as hallucinations.
Suddenly, a young man stepped out of the shadows:
I was not terrified, as I might have been at home.

Besides, he was smiling & gentle as you used to be.
'A kiss' he pleads 'a kiss' in soft Portuguese.
I quickened my step, but he padded behind me.

He looked so young, my heart went out to him.
I stopped in the shadows under the Cathedral.
We kissed, and the tears poured down my face.

SHE CRIES

She puts her face against the wall
and cries, crying for herself,
crying for our children, crying
for all of us
                    in this strange age
of shrinking space, with the needle
of Concorde saluting Mount Gabriel
with its supersonic boom, soaring
from London or Paris to Washington,
a slender, metallic, flying swan

& all the other paraphernalia, hidden
missiles hoarding in silos, bloated
astronauts striding the dusty moon,
and far beyond, our lonely message,
the long probe towards Venus

but most of all for her husband
she cries, against the wall,
the poet at his wooden desk,
that toad with a jewel in his head,
no longer privileged, but still
trying to crash, without faltering,
the sound barrier, the dying word.

CLEAR THE WAY

Jimmy Drummond used bad language at school
All the four-letter words, like a drip from a drain.
At six he knew how little children were born
As well he might, since his mother bore nine,
Six after her soldier husband left for the wars

Under the motto of the Royal Irish, *Clear the Way!*
When his body returned from England
The authorities told them not to unscrew the lid
To see the remnants of Fusilier Drummond inside –
A chancey hand-grenade had left nothing to hide

And Jimmy's mother was pregnant at the graveside –
Clear the way, and nothing to hide.
Love came to her punctually each springtide,
Settled in the ditch under some labouring man:
'It comes over you, you have to lie down.'

Her only revenge on her hasty lovers
Was to call each child after its father,
Which the locals admired, and seeing her saunter
To collect the pension of her soldier husband
Trailed by her army of baby Irregulars.

Some of whom made soldiers for future wars
Some supplied factories in England.
Jimmy Drummond was the eldest but died younger than any
When he fell from a scaffolding in Coventry
Condemned, like all his family, to *Clear the Way!*

THE HAG OF BEARE

Ebb tide has come for me:
My life drifts downwards
Like a retreating sea
With no tidal turn.

I am the Hag of Beare,
Fine petticoats I used to wear,
Today, gaunt with poverty,
I hunt for rags to cover me.

Girls nowadays
Dream only of money –
When we were young
We cared more for our men.

Riding over their lands
We remember how, like gentlemen,
They treated us well;
Courted, but didn't tell.

Today every upstart
Is a master of graft;
Skinflint, yet sure to boast
Of being a lavish host.

But I bless my King who gave –
Balanced briefly on time's wave –
Largesse of speedy chariots
And champion thoroughbreds.

These arms, now bony, thin
And useless to younger men,
Once caressed with skill
The limbs of princes!

Sadly my body seeks to join
Them soon in their dark home –
When God wishes to claim it,
He can have back his deposit.

No more love-teasing
For me, no wedding feast:
Scant grey hair is best
Shadowed by a veil.

Why should I care?
Many's the bright scarf
Adorned my hair in the days
When I drank with the gentry.

So God be praised
That I misspent my days!
Whether the plunge be bold
Or timid, the blood runs cold.

After spring and autumn
Come age's frost and body's chill:
Even in bright sunlight
I carry my shawl.

Lovely the mantle of green
Our Lord spreads on the hillside!
Every spring the divine craftsman
Plumps its worn fleece.

But my cloak is mottled with age –
No, I'm beginning to dote –
It's only grey hair straggling
Over my skin, a lichened oak.

And my right eye has been taken away
As down payment on heaven's estate;
Likewise the ray in the left
That I may grope to heaven's gate.

No storm has overthrown
The royal standing stone.
Every year the fertile plain
Bears its crop of yellow grain.

But I, who feasted royally
By candlelight, now pray
In this darkened oratory.
Instead of heady mead

And wine, high on the bench
With kings, I sup whey
In a nest of hags:
God pity me!

Yet may this cup of whey
O! Lord, serve as my ale-feast –
Fathoming its bitterness
I'll learn that you know best.

Alas, I cannot
Again sail youth's sea;
The days of my beauty
Are departed, and desire spent.

I hear the fierce cry of the wave
Whipped by the wintry wind.
No one will visit me today
Neither nobleman nor slave.

I hear their phantom oars
As ceaselessly they row
And row to the chill ford,
Or fall asleep by its side.

Flood tide
And the ebb dwindling on the sand!
What the flood rides ashore
The ebb snatches from your hand.

Flood tide
And the sucking ebb to follow!
Both I have come to know
Pouring down my body.

Flood tide
Has not yet rifled my pantry
But a chill hand has been laid
On many who in darkness visited me.

Well might the Son of Mary
Take their place under my roof-tree
For if I lack other hospitality
I never say 'No' to anybody –

Man being of all
Creatures the most miserable –
His flooding pride always seen
But never his tidal turn.

Happy the island in mid-ocean
Washed by the returning flood
But my ageing blood
Slows to final ebb.

I have hardly a dwelling
Today, on this earth.
Where once was life's flood
All is ebb.

after the early Irish

At the least touch of your fingertips
I break into blossom,
my whole chemical composition
transformed.
I sprawl like a grassy meadow
fragrant in the sun;
at the brush of your palm, all my herbs
and spices spill open

frond by frond, lured to unfold
and exhale in the heat;
wild strawberries rife, and pimpernels
flagrant and scarlet, blushing
down their stems.
To mow that rushy bottom;
sweet scything.

All winter I waited silently
for your appeal.
I withered within, dead to all,
curled away, and deaf as clay,
all my life forces ebbing slowly
till now I come to, at your touch,
revived as from a death swoon.

Your sun lightens my sky
and a wind lifts, like God's angel,
to move the waters,
every inch of me quivers

before your presence,
goose-pimples I get as you glide
over me, and every hair
stands on end.

Hours later I linger
in the ladies toilet,
a sweet scent wafting
from all my pores,
proof positive, if a sign
was needed, that at the least
touch of your fingertips
I break into blossom.

after the Irish of Nuala Ní Dhomhnaill

THE DEATH OF ACTEON

Who plays in the dark glitter of the running streams?

When he saw her naked breasts did he want to die?
And was she so cruel, woman or goddess,
that she wanted to hurl him out of his body?

To desire is to perish into strange skies.

But the surge of her blood had not
come to the point where she would want
him to see her, to advance, to assault.
'Lower your glance, Acteon. Let others ...
I'll leave you for the dogs' swears the Goddess

settling into the spectacle demanded by her fury.

For life's law is always intransigent
if you live by the quest, the attempt to possess.
A golden body gilding the darkness,
a tall pale torso, with arrows erect,
in the trampled foliage of the night.
And further on she dawns ... a warrior queen
for days, for whole countries, unseizable.

– I sought or fled her;
I carried her everywhere.

From where I stood her tracks began,
tracks crisscrossed by her wanderings.
To attain her I waded through marshes, low mists
and both sides of the abyss
I leaped in a bound, believing her there.

Scenting her trail, I mistook my way,
raging and ranting against the world,
until I suddenly found her. No longer astray
I approach slowly, slipping through the thicket.
My faun's yellow eyes peer
through the shifting leaves to devour her,
giant huntress!

She steps into the water with her maidens.
Skirts kirtled up, they frolic in the chaste
clear springs. Limbs lift in the blue spray.
The water reflects the mackerel sky.

Then she saw my desire, met my eyes.
Her embarrassed rage struck the forest,
reached the rocks, the gorges & undergrowth: –
the whole landscape suspended, shimmering.
She hesitates a moment, relieved or lost,
and I believe ... advance, goddess conqueror!

In the trough where she displays her open thighs
she holds her spear aloft. She might
have cut me down there, impure and untouchable

and halted Acteon in his tracks forever.
but anxious to miss nothing,
to savor her pleasure, she slows his suffering,
seized in the unwinding of her spell.

... All of a sudden his face is youthful,
his gaze has become simple and doleful.
A crest of antlers enlarges his brow.
Fur spreads over his legs, already sprouting hooves.
And the bones, one by one, are dissolved,
the knees, the hands, the membranes –
the blood heats through shocked tissue.

Still enough of him left to recognize the man.
The bristling fury of his hounds reawakens
his hunter's passion, kindled in vain;
he pities the stag which he is becoming:
the stag he has brought to bay so often.
Stale scraps soon ... meanwhile neighbors
sharing a skin. What terrible complicity
approaches with each warm heartbeat
as the first dogs, growing bold, growl?
Horror stricken, Acteon watches, joins in.

From the other shore, one foot stirring the water,
Diane watches, showing her women
the motionless Acteon
who, despite his new dress, interests himself
in the hounds which scent, then draw back from him.

The death that gave him his own body
he now sees returning, to accomplish its destiny,
preparing the feast of his changing flesh.
Terrible and calm, life's wet nurse,
our single mother, shows him a last sign ...

... What *was* the quest? The adversary
is all that manages to escape.
The exit is not the human mouth
but the underground passage.
Become the one I chase, I am lost.
The Other is death. I learn
as I begin to forget;
penetrated by darkness, relieved of myself,
ravished, given over to the unknown.

What did he see that he shouldn't?
Was the abandon of your body, reflected in his eyes,
so hateful to you, warrior queen?

A body to ravish, to brandish, to charm: everything.
The Great Mother, endlessly teeming.
Untamed, common property, at peril, ecstatic,
ancient cleft hidden under the leaves.
The gaping fall of the wound. Swelling mountain.
Burning, burning with joy to discover together
a unique body, its shining splendor.

– Is it a woman he grips
in the fangs that tear at him?
Through those furious mouths does she
caress, for once, his conquered body?
... Naked the goddess, naked the thousand beasts,
naked the desire which rips and rends him!

Now the debate is between the dogs and himself,
and death waits in the icecold thicket.
A rock, seen through stag eyes, distracts him.
Howling and belling, a hurling clamor
has become his voice's echo.
He flounders among his cries.
He gives up his limbs to the greedy.
Within the walls of his distraught body
he is already stumbling towards the hidden passage:
the hellish barking, he recognizes:
innocent victims, cruel beasts. O Faithful
hounds of youth! The pack that had
always devoured him was himself.

He is not dead yet, he still dies, he is struck down
dreaming
of his implacable, always unsatisfied lust,
of all his past
that those fabulous beasts pass from mouth to mouth.
A spring of fresh blood for lapping tongues,

his own dogs' daily food.
Black words, welling up through
his last breath, under the tooth of Cerberus:
shreds of stifled denials
soon swallowed.

– *Could a mere glance offend a goddess?*

The always plunging stream, the spreading pool,
the two neat islands, the pleasant frolicking
of the nymphs, the pale folds of their tunics,
the measured shadows on the rippling water
gather to the silent smile of a dance.

after André Frénaud

When we have once seen happiness shining on the face of a person we love, we know that there can be no other vocation for man except to bring this light into the faces which surround us . . . and we are torn apart at the thought of the sadness and night which, by the very fact of being alive, we cast into the hearts we meet.

CAMUS